THE MEDIEVAL MONASTERY

Roger Rosewell

SHIRE PUBLICATIONS

Published in Great Britain in 2012 by Shire Publications Ltd,
Midland House, West Way, Botley, Oxford OX2 0PH,
United Kingdom.

44-02 23rd Street, Suite 219, Long Island City, NY 11101,
USA.

E-mail: shire@shirebooks.co.uk   www.shirebooks.co.uk

© 2012 Roger Rosewell.

Every attempt has been made by the Publishers to secure
the appropriate permissions for materials reproduced in
this book. If there has been any oversight we will be happy
to rectify the situation and a written submission should be
made to the Publishers.

A CIP catalogue record for this book is available from the
British Library.

Shire Library no. 687.   ISBN-13: 978 0 74781 146 6

Roger Rosewell has asserted his right under the
Copyright, Designs and Patents Act, 1988, to be identified
as the author of this book.

Designed by Tony Truscott Designs, Sussex, UK
and typeset in Perpetua and Gill Sans.

Printed in China through Worldprint Ltd.

12 13 14 15 16   10 9 8 7 6 5 4 3 2 1

COVER IMAGE
St Bernard arriving at Clairvaux with his monks,
fifteenth-century manuscript © The British Library,
Yates Thompson Ms 32, f.9v.

TITLE PAGE IMAGE
The chapter-house vestibule of Chester Abbey
(Benedictine: now Chester Cathedral), thirteenth century.

DEDICATION
To the people of Yelford parish.

THANKS
Matthew Champion, Peter Fullerton, Susan Harrison,
Christine Huddleston, Annie Janik, Cameron Newham,
Lyn Stilgoe and Robin Wiltshire.

ACKNOWLEDGEMENTS
Photographs appear by kind permission of the Dean and
Chapter of the cathedrals of Canterbury, Chester,
Gloucester, St Albans, Winchester and Worcester and the
Chapter of Ely Cathedral; the Vicar and churchwardens
of Malvern Priory and Tewkesbury Abbey; the Rector
and churchwardens of Binham Priory, Hexham Abbey,
Leominster Priory and Pershore Abbey. Gratitude is also
extended to English Heritage and Cadw. Thanks also to the
following copyright holders: The British Library, cover,
pages 10 (top), 14, 15, and 33; Canterbury Cathedral
Archives, page 55; Martin Crampin, page 61; Peter
Edwards, pages 36, 42 (bottom), 43 (bottom), 48
(bottom), and 51; Annie Janik Studio, page 18 (bottom);
Aidan McCrea Thompson, page 18; National Portrait
Gallery, page 68 (top); C. B. Newham, pages 6–7; 11,
21 (bottom), 23 (top and bottom); 39, and 46. 70–1;
Reading Local Studies Library, page 18 (top); The Dean
and Chapter of Winchester Cathedral, pages 8
and 24 (assigned by the author). All other images are
the author's own.

Shire Publications is supporting the Woodland Trust, the UK's leading woodland conservation charity, by funding the dedication of trees.

CONTENTS

INTRODUCTION

FOR NEARLY A THOUSAND YEARS, religiously devout men and women in medieval Britain joined monasteries in the hope that, if they separated themselves from others and followed the words of Jesus in the Bible – 'Everyone that hath forsaken houses, or brethren or lands for my name's sake' – they would find 'everlasting life'.

This book explores the purpose of those monasteries and describes the daily life of monks and nuns. It explains the differences between the four Monastic Orders (Benedictine, Cluniac, Carthusian and Cistercian), and outlines how monasteries were designed and managed. Separate chapters focus on nunneries and the various quasi-monastic orders. The book concludes with an account of the Dissolution of the Monasteries and a gazetteer where medieval abbeys and priories can be visited today.

The first monks were third-century Christian hermits in North Africa who sought a contemplative life in desert caves or mud huts until they began to form small communities (monasteries) for mutual protection and support. In Britain the earliest recorded of these monastery-type settlements date from the fifth century at Tintagel (Cornwall), Wales as early as AD 500 and Scotland in AD 563 when monks from Ireland colonised Iona, a small island off the west coast in the Inner Hebrides.

The arrival of Italian priests in England on a papal mission to convert the Anglo-Saxons to Christianity and their subsequent founding of a monastery church at Canterbury (Kent) around AD 597 redirected those efforts and laid the foundations for the great abbeys of medieval Britain.

Enriched by lavish donations from pious kings and landowners, by the sixteenth century

their successors had amassed huge estates and owned around twenty-five per cent of England and Wales.

While their spiritual motivations may have been similar, the lives of monks towards the end of the Middle Ages were considerably more comfortable than those of their predecessors who had entered monasteries three hundred

Above:
Fifteenth-century
tomb effigy of
King Athelstan
(d. AD 939),
who endowed
Malmesbury Abbey
(Benedictine:
Wiltshire).

years earlier. Paradoxically, such wealth also made them dangerously vulnerable when the clamour of the protestant Reformation merged with the avarice of Henry VIII (reigned 1509–47). The upshot was a wave of upheaval and change that saw all but one of the kingdom's monasteries dissolved in 1540 – their buildings sold, their inhabitants evicted, their buildings reduced to what William Shakespeare (1564–1616) called 'bare ruined choirs'.

Byland Abbey ruins (Cistercian: Yorkshire), built in the thirteenth century. Note the remains of the mosaic tile pavement.

THE FOUR MONASTIC ORDERS

BETWEEN THE SIXTH AND TWELFTH CENTURIES, a variety of monastic networks evolved across Europe which eventually consolidated into four main Orders or organisations. Those monasteries ruled by an abbot were called abbeys; those governed by a subordinate prior, priories.

THE BENEDICTINES (BLACK MONKS)

By far the largest and wealthiest of these Orders were the Benedictines. They took their name from a set of rules for communal living which had been adapted from an earlier text by the sixth-century Italian abbot, St Benedict of Nursia (c.480–c.547). These rules – the *Regula Benedicti* – spelled out how monks should spend their time between spiritual and physical work, what they should eat, what clothing they should wear, and much more. The rules were simultaneously humane, devout, practical ... and very demanding: a framework not just for daily living but an act of submission which defined the essence of monastic life itself. They were called Black monks after the colour of their loose-fitting tunics (habits) which symbolised humility.

Many monasteries added to the *Regula Benedicti* by producing their own books of customs and rules known as 'customaries', prescribing procedures for every contingency: what should happen if a monk had a nose-bleed during a service, how a monk should tidy his bed after getting up, how a diner should hold a cup, for example.

Although Benedictine ideas were known in England from at least the seventh century, none of the first wave of Anglo-Saxon monasteries such as St Augustine's Canterbury (Kent), Glastonbury (Somerset), Malmesbury (Wiltshire) and Wearmouth/Jarrow (Northumbria) followed St Benedict's edicts to the letter. Other customs and traditions also thrived, in part because these monasteries were also important institutions in the life of the church and of the kings, who provided their land and wealth. Many became important centres for the preservation, study and dissemination of classical and Christian culture.

Such lavish patronage inevitably made monasteries irresistible targets when Viking pirates launched repeated raids on Britain between the eighth

Opposite: Detail of a Benedictine monk on the tomb of Bishop William Wykeham (d. 1404), Winchester Cathedral Priory (Benedictine: Hampshire).

and tenth centuries. The first to suffer was Lindisfarne on the Northumbrian coast, which was plundered in AD 793. Over the next century scores of others were burned and looted; some were completely wiped out. Jarrow was ransacked in the late ninth century and remained a ruin for two hundred years.

The restoration of social order in the tenth century saw the revival of some of the

Above: St Benedict delivers the Rule, from the *Rule of St Benedict* at the Monastery of St Gilles in Nîmes, France, 1129.

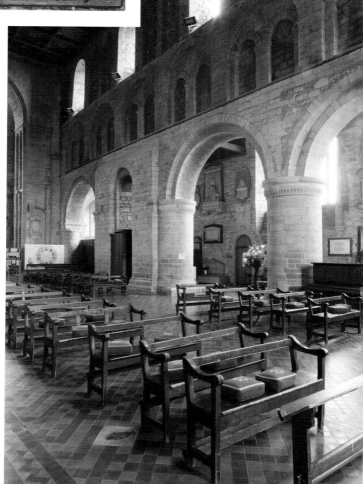

The twelfth-century nave at Leominster Priory (Benedictine: Herefordshire).

monasteries devastated during the invasions of the previous century. At Glastonbury a new generation of monks formally embraced the continental European model of Benedictine rules as the basis of their lives and built a monastery which included a cloister, the first time this distinctive architectural feature seems to have been adopted in Britain.

On the eve of the Norman Conquest in 1066 there was a loose network of about forty of these new-style Benedictine monasteries in England, all south of the River Trent, many owning large estates and having close links to the royal family. Three were attached to adjacent cathedrals: Canterbury, Winchester and Worcester. After the Conquest the number of Benedictine monasteries increased as members of the new regime imported monks from France, rebuilt abbeys such as Gloucester, and created others, at Shrewsbury and elsewhere. Additional cathedral priories were also established at Bath, Coventry, Durham, Ely, Norwich and Rochester. In the thirteenth century these monasteries became part of the newly formed international Benedictine Order.

The west front of Castle Acre Priory (Cluniac: Norfolk), c. 1160.

THE CLUNIACS

The second Monastic Order also followed the *Regula Benedicti* but took its name from the extremely wealthy abbey of Cluny in central France to which it owed ultimate obedience. Cluniac monks differed from others in that they devoted most of their day to prayer. Thirty-five Cluniac priories were founded in England after the Norman Conquest; the first was at Lewes (Sussex), *c*. 1081. Impressive remains of others survive at Castle Acre (Norfolk) and Wenlock (Shropshire).

Although favoured by royal patrons, like other 'alien' priories which had close links with France, their loyalty was questioned during the Hundred Years War (1337–1453). In the fourteenth and fifteenth centuries the larger Cluniac houses repudiated their French origins by putting themselves under English control.

The other two Monastic Orders were led by men who wanted to revive the original purity of monasticism as conceived in the third and fifth centuries with the

Detail of a fifteenth-century wall painting of the Crucifixion in the former refectory of the Carthusian Charterhouse of St Anne, Coventry (Warwickshire).

emphasis on work, frugality, and private communion with God. They disliked the comfortable lifestyles of typical Benedictine monasteries, especially Cluny, where the monks consorted with royalty and had built a vast church filled with lavish artworks. The first cracks appeared in Italy where complaints were voiced about the 'protracted chanting of hymns', the 'unnecessary sounding of bells' and the 'conspicuous use of ornaments', but when the same criticisms spread to France the consequences were even more far-reaching, dividing existing monastic communities and spawning a wave of new 'reforming' orders.

THE CARTHUSIANS

Around 1080 a group of monks who wanted to recreate the seclusion of the early desert hermits formed a small community in the French alpine area of Chartreuse. Its members lived in individual 'cells' where they ate, prayed and slept alone, coming together only a few times a day for common services. Known as Carthusians, after Chartreuse, they eventually founded nine monasteries – usually called Charterhouses rather than abbeys – in England. The first was in a royal forest at Witham (Somerset), described by one disgruntled late-twelfth-century monk as, 'a horrible place, an empty solitude, inhabited only by wild animals'. Although few in number these monks were widely admired for the unbending rigour of their religious observances. In the 1390s a monk from Rochester quit the London Charterhouse, wailing, 'I cannot bear the discipline of the order'.

THE CISTERCIANS (WHITE MONKS)

A more important breakaway occurred in 1098 when a group of French monks left the prosperous Benedictine abbey of Molesme in central Burgundy to form a 'new' monastery in the wilderness at Cîteaux (Latin: Cistercium), near Dijon. Like the Carthusians they too wanted to rediscover the purity and denial of early monasticism, but as a community rather than as semi-hermits. After an offshoot or 'daughter' abbey had been founded at nearby Clairvaux by one of its most charismatic leaders, St Bernard (1090–1153), a set of guidelines was issued ensuring that any new houses observed the same practices and rules as the founder; in effect creating the Cistercians, the first fully-fledged monastic Order in the medieval church. Under these statutes, each new abbey received an annual visit or inspection ('visitation') by the abbot of the mother-house, and all abbots were to meet each year at Cîteaux for a parliament of abbots called the 'general chapter'. Unlike traditional Benedictine monks, the Cistercians wore white habits, the plain bleached wool emphasising their vows of poverty. One author said they resembled 'a flock of sea-gulls' (see cover illustration).

Within a relatively short period the zeal of the Cistercians had radically changed the course of Western monasticism, inspiring a surge of similar foundations across Europe. In 1128 they established their first abbey in England at Waverley, near Ripley (Surrey), and their second (the first in Wales) at Tintern (Monmouthshire) in 1131. Soon a trickle became a stream, with Rievaulx and Fountains, both in Yorkshire, following shortly afterwards and Melrose in Scotland in 1136. In 1147 a similar, but smaller 'reforming' order known as the Savignacs, after the French Abbey of Savigny, merged with the Cistercians, bringing abbeys such as Furness (Cumbria) and Buildwas (Shropshire) into the Cîteaux fold.

By the late Middle Ages, however, many of the initial differences between the Cistercians and the Benedictines, such as conflicting opinions about the role of art in churches, had mellowed.

Stained glass panel, c. 1505–20, showing St Bernard (kneeling) being appointed to found the Abbey of Clairvaux. It was originally made for the cloisters of Altenberg Abbey (Cistercian: Germany), but is now in the church of St Mary, Shrewsbury (Shropshire).

BECOMING A MONK

BEFORE THE THIRTEENTH CENTURY there were several ways in which people could become a monk. While some joined as adults, others had little choice: having been raised in monasteries since childhood after their parents had made an offering or 'oblation' of them to the abbot. At Winchester Cathedral Priory (Benedictine: Hampshire), for example, thirty-five of forty-one new recruits who joined the monastery between the mid-1030s and 1072 were boys (*pueri*). Once enrolled it was almost impossible for them to leave – where would they go; what other life did they know? Elsewhere in Europe many influential figures in Benedictine monasticism were former oblates. They included Abbess Hildegard of Bingen (1098–1179), oblated at the age of eight, and Abbot Suger of Saint-Denis (1081–1151), oblated at ten; the latter now best known for his patronage of gothic architecture at the famous royal abbey of Saint-Denis, north of Paris.

Around 1200, however, this system had largely disappeared from English male monasteries. The main reasons seem to have been a switch in aristocratic interests from monasteries to churches and assorted misgivings about the role of children in solemn places.

For adults the different Orders imposed different entry conditions. The first was age. The Cistercians insisted on a minimum age of sixteen, Benedictines about the same and the Carthusians twenty-one. Some monks joined monasteries when they were much older. At Byland Abbey (Cistercian: Yorkshire), for example, one of the thirteenth-century monks was a former bishop, pirate and

A boy oblate being received into a monastery, from a fourteenth-century *Decretum* (Book of Canon or Church law).

adventurer who seemed to enjoy nothing more than regaling his fellow brethren with accounts of 'his most audacious acts as well as his merited misfortunes'. Others were priests.

Social class was important. Although in theory there were no distinctions between nobles or paupers, in practice St Benedict understood the value of attracting recruits from the social and political elites and the benefits that their money and influence brought. When wealthy patrons endowed monasteries they often reserved the rights to nominate candidates and to appoint family members or allies to key posts. Even when these ties slackened, admission was restricted. From the fourteenth century until the Dissolution male monasteries required a fixed fee of £5 from novices for the cost of their clothing (habit); a sum beyond the resources of poorer people. As life as a monk demanded fluency in Latin, either learned before admission or acquired in a monastic school, such requirements again excluded most of the population, irrespective of their religious inclinations. In the late Middle Ages some prestigious monasteries even demanded references from potential recruits. Novices served a probationary period ranging from a few weeks or months to a year during which they were introduced to monastic life and given time to accustom themselves to its disciplines and routines. In larger monasteries, novices had their own quarters where they studied religious texts and were taught singing. Other parts of the curriculum included learning the customaries of the house and the system of sign language that could be used when silence was mandatory, as at mealtimes. At Canterbury Cathedral Priory novices had to pass examinations in Latin grammar, logic, and philosophy before they could 'profess' their vows of obedience, chastity and poverty.

Monk being given a tonsure, from *De similitudinibus*, c. 1220.

Admission to any Order saw new monks given the tonsure — a symbolic shaving of the head imitating the crown of thorns worn by Christ during his Crucifixion. At Eynsham Abbey (Benedictine: Oxfordshire), the experience went further; new recruits were ordered not to lower the hood (cowl) of their habit for three days until their heads were ceremonially uncovered and they emerged, like Christ from his entombment, into the light of their rebirth as servants of God.

Thereafter any who attempted to run away would be hunted, found, returned and punished.

THE ARCHITECTURE
OF MONASTERIES

BY THE ELEVENTH CENTURY a typical monastery consisted of a church with attached living quarters for the monks, guest accommodation for visitors, and a mixture of associated buildings including workshops and stores. Proximity to water was essential.

The scale and condition of these buildings depended on the size and wealth of the monastery. The interiors of Benedictine and Cluniac churches were richly decorated with painted statues, stained glass windows and altar fittings of gold and silver. Beauty was seen as a way of serving and honouring God. Many of these churches had three or more semi-circular apses at the eastern end providing an arc of radiating chapels. They could also be of cathedral-size proportions. The abbey church at Bury St Edmunds (Benedictine: Suffolk) was 505 feet long and 200 feet wide. The Cluniac church of St Pancras at Lewes Priory (East Sussex), built in the twelfth and thirteenth centuries, was 420 feet long from west door to chancel apse, with an internal vault height of 93 feet at the altar and 105 feet at the crossing.

Early Cistercian churches, by contrast, while of similar size, were simpler, more austere buildings. Although expensive building materials and techniques could be used, opulent fittings such as coloured glass, carpets, wallhangings and paintings were initially prohibited as wasteful and incompatible with an aesthetic taste that equated plain interiors with the purity of Christ. By the thirteenth century, however, such injunctions were beginning to crumble.

The size of monastic communities also varied considerably. Thus while the Cathedral Priory at Canterbury (Benedictine: Kent) and Rievaulx Abbey (Cistercian: Yorkshire) both had around 140 monks in the late twelfth century, others barely mustered a minimum of twelve (after the twelve apostles). Carthusian houses were always relatively small. The largest, at Sheen (Surrey), had only thirty monks.

Typical monasteries were built around two courts, each entered by a separate gatehouse. The first, outer court, housed agricultural and industrial buildings such as stables, watermills, barns, dovecotes, tanneries, smiths'

Opposite:
Fan vaulting
in the east
cloister alley at
Gloucester Abbey
(Benedictine:
now Gloucester
Cathedral), dating
from the third
quarter of the
fourteenth century.

forges, and various ponds and meadows. Those belonging to the Cistercians tended to be more extensive as they were built in rural locations and sought total self-sufficiency. The buildings, gardens and ponds of the outer court or precincts of Rievaulx Abbey covered an area of about 90 acres.

The inner court contained the heart of the monastery: the church and the monks' cloister. Access to this area was restricted, and the gatehouse (some of which were fortified) represented a boundary between two worlds, physical and mental. A monk needed permission to leave this area, and women were generally not allowed to enter. The hub of a monk's life was a

The inner gateway of Reading Abbey (Cluniac: Berkshire) before restoration. Photograph by W. H. Fox Talbot, c. 1840–9.

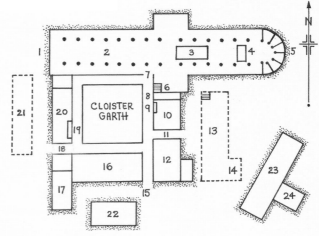

Plan of a typical Benedictine monastery.

1 West end of church	10 Chapter house	17 Kitchen
2 Nave	11 Parlour/slype to	18 West parlour
3 Choir (Quire)	infirmary	19 Laver
4 High altar	12 Day room	20 Undercroft/cellars
5 Chapels	13 Dormitory above	21 Abbot's lodgings
6 Night stairs	the east range	above west range
7 Monks' entrance to	14 Latrines	22 Guest house
the church	15 Entrance to the	23 Infirmary
8 Sacristy or parlour	cloisters	24 Infirmary chapel
9 Book cupboard	16 Refectory	

four-sided cloister arranged around a square or rectangular courtyard known as the 'garth'. At Rochester Cathedral Priory (Benedictine: Kent) the fourteenth-century accounts record regular payments for mowing this area.

Cloisters were simultaneously thoroughfares and working spaces, used for study, for novice classes, for washing and shaving, and for ritualised processions. Their alleys provided doors or staircases leading to the church and the other rooms: a large meeting room known as the chapter house, a parlour, a dormitory where the monks slept (*dorter*), the latrines, a washing area (*lavatorium*), a refectory where meals were served (*frater*), the kitchen, a day room (sometimes called the *calefactorium*, or warming room), the abbot's private rooms or lodgings, and other spaces essential for monastic life such as an outer parlour for receiving visitors, and 'slypes' or passages leading to a separate infirmary building and the cemetery. To contemporary eyes the largest of these complexes would have resembled the palaces and the estates of wealthy aristocrats.

Carthusian monasteries followed a different pattern from the others. As their members sought to emulate the solitude of desert hermits they largely shunned the traditional communal life, preferring to reside in individual small houses organised around a large cloister which included a chapter house but not a dormitory.

The cloister garth at Worcester Cathedral Priory (Benedictine: Worcester).

Right: The monks' door from the cloister to the church at Tewkesbury Abbey (Benedictine: Gloucestershire), built in the fifteenth century.

Far right: The west parlour of Gloucester Abbey (Benedictine: now Gloucester Cathedral).

The chapter house at Buildwas Abbey (Cistercian: Shropshire), with a section of surviving tiled floor, dates from the third quarter of the twelfth century.

Apart from the claustral range, monasteries also included a *hospitium* or guest house and the almonry, a building usually near the gates, where alms or gifts such as food, clothing, and money were given to the poor. Accurate information about the level of alms-giving is patchy. Estimates

ranging from 3 to 10 per cent of monastic income have been suggested. During the famine of 1194–6 Fountains Abbey and other Cistercian monasteries in Yorkshire established refugee camps at their gates. On other occasions, however, the same abbeys refused to help the able-bodied poor during harvest seasons, arguing that they had plenty of opportunities to find work.

Fourteenth-century carving of a monk with bread and ale, at Muchelney Abbey (Benedictine: Somerset).

Hospitality was an essential component of monastic life, and guest accommodation was provided by every Order, including the Carthusians. Most guests seemed to have stayed just for a few days but sometimes monastic finances were badly damaged by the costs of entertaining large parties. Hospitality was often socially stratified with important guests staying in the abbot's lodgings or similar high-status buildings, while middle-ranking visitors were housed in the *hospitium* and poorer travellers relegated to the almonry.

Some monasteries also provided accommodation for 'corrodians', lay people who lived in the complex.

The church and ruins of Mount Grace Priory (Carthusian: Yorkshire). The surviving foundations show the layout of Carthusian monks' cells.

MANAGING A MONASTERY

M ANAGING an important monastery required a team of senior departmental managers, professional aides and large numbers of servants.

Most monasteries were ruled by an abbot (Latin *abbas*: father) who was ultimately responsible for its household and financial affairs and to whom the monks owed obedience. He was assisted by a range of office holders called obedientiaries including a deputy (the prior), the novicemaster, the cellarer who was in charge of supplies, the chamberlain who looked after domestic matters, the sacrist who was responsible for the upkeep of the church, the precentor who directed the church services, the infirmarer who cared for the sick, and the almoner who administered the charitable side of the monastery's work. In addition, senior monks known as roundsmen or *circatores* patrolled the complex ensuring that nobody was misbehaving or neglecting the Rule. The precise number, titles and duties of obedientaries varied from monastery to monastery. At Bury St Edmunds Abbey (Benedictine: Suffolk) there were four priors. At Durham Cathedral Priory (Benedictine: Durham) and Canterbury Cathedral Priory there were twenty-five major officials, some with subordinates. It is estimated that by the end of the Middle Ages as many as two thirds of monks in a typical monastery held office as obedientaries or as their deputies. Some monks received practical training in administrative skills, including bookkeeping. In many instances such officials were often excused part of their choir duties and eventually lived separately from ordinary 'choir monks'.

Cistercian abbeys were organised along broadly similar lines to the Benedictine monasteries, except that the porter of a Cistercian abbey would be responsible for distributing alms to the poor and the post of almoner did not exist.

Effigy of Abbot Parker (d. 1539), the last Abbot of Gloucester Abbey (Benedictine: now Gloucester Cathedral).

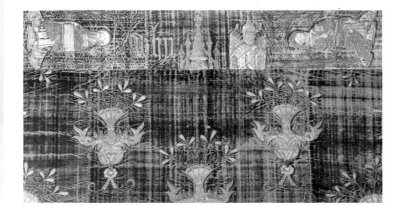

Embroidered cope with the letters 'WHY' and a church; the rebus of William Whitchurch, Abbot of Hailes Abbey, 1464–79 (Cistercian: Gloucestershire). The cope is now in the parish church of St Michael, Buckland (Gloucestershire).

In some instances monasteries were ruled by a prior rather than an abbot. This happened when monasteries were 'cells' of, or subordinate to, more important abbeys, or in monasteries attached to cathedrals where the bishop was nominally in charge.

Many abbots (or priors) commissioned major building programmes and lavish works of art for their monasteries. The Cistercians have been called the missionaries of French Gothic architecture in northern England while elaborate fan vaulting was pioneered by the Benedictines at Gloucester Abbey (see page 16). Some abbots 'signed' the works of art they commissioned with their initials.

Monasteries depended on their income from tithes, rents, donations, services and traded goods. Monks were highly protective of these 'rights' and clashes with other landowners, tenants and townspeople were common. For example, on several occasions in the late fifteenth century, monks at Chester Abbey (Benedictine: now Chester Cathedral) were indicted in the mayor's court for attacks on local citizens and in 1480 Abbot Richard Oldham and twelve others, of whom at least half can be identified as monks, were bound over to keep the peace with a large body of tradesmen. Not all monasteries were well managed: some abbots were weak and lax; a few possibly corrupt. Debt was a common problem; the description of a twelfth-century abbot at Bury St Edmunds – 'pious and kindly, strict and good, but in the business of this world neither good nor wise' – could have applied to many others.

Fragment of oak screen dated 1536 with the initials 'A. S.' (Adam of Sedbar or Sedbergh, Abbot of Jervaulx Abbey (Cistercian: Yorkshire) 1533–7. The screen is now in the parish church of St Andrew, Aysgarth (Yorkshire). Adam was executed in 1537.

DAILY LIFE I:
PRAYER, STUDY, WORK

APART FROM EATING, sleeping, washing, and short spells of private relaxation, the core of a monk's life was a daily routine of liturgical devotion, interspersed with periods set aside for spiritual reading and manual work designed to prevent idleness and distractions. St Benedict called these periods *opus Dei* (God's work), *lectio divina* (religious reading/study) and *labora* (labour/work).

OPUS DEI

By the beginning of the twelfth century each of the Four Orders divided their time between *opus Dei*, *lectio* and *labora* in different ways. Most monks spent a high proportion of their daytime hours in cycles of prayer, readings from the Bible and recitations from the Book of Psalms (Psalter), a collection of songs of thanksgiving and praise, and pleas for help from God. These cycles consisted of seven daytime services known as the Canonical Hours or Offices, each held a couple of hours apart and inspired by Psalm 119:164, *Seven times a day do I praise thee*. The first service began at daybreak with Lauds, followed by Prime, Terce, Sext, None, Vespers, and Compline at sunset. An eighth office of Vigils was celebrated at night. Over the course of the Middle Ages some of these services were known by different names. Lauds was once called Matins and what was then called Nocturns or Vigils is now known as Matins. In the late fifteenth century Matins and Lauds were together referred to as Vigils.

As a monk's day was regulated by the sun, beginning at dawn and finishing at sunset, the timing of these services differed according to the seasons of the year. Before the invention of mechanical clocks in the thirteenth century, the time-tabling of services relied on water clocks and astronomy for accuracy. In keeping with their solitary life the Carthusians only came together in the church for Vigils, Lauds and Vespers, the remaining offices being recited in their individual cells.

Services were sung in an enclosed area at the eastern end of the church known as the Choir (alternative spelling: Quire), directly west of the

CISTERCIAN TIMETABLE (WINTER)

2.30 a.m.	Rise	Noon	Sext
3.30 a.m.	Vigils		Mass
6.00 a.m.	Lauds	1.30 p.m.	None
	Prime		Dinner
	Reading		Work
8.00 a.m.	Terce	4.15 p.m.	Vespers
	Mass		Reading
	Chapter-house	6.15	Compline
	meeting	6.30	Bed time
	Work		

Effigy of Hugh le Despenser (d. 1348), Tewkesbury Abbey (Benedictine: Gloucestershire). The Despenser family were the founders of the Abbey.

high altar (presbytery) and separated from the nave by a solid screen, known as the *pulpitum*, which provided privacy and protection from draughts. Monks entered the church in procession from the east alley of the cloister in order of seniority, which was calculated by their length of service or rank rather than by age.

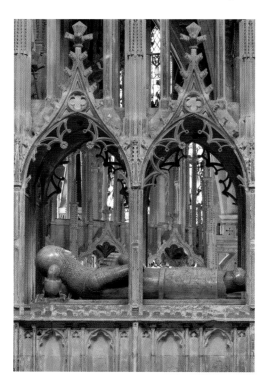

Monks were expected to take these services seriously, avoiding lateness or singing too fast. Early Cistercians particularly disapproved of 'swelling and swooping' voices, which 'mocked' the gravity of worship. While these misdemeanours were easy to recognise and punish, policing stray thoughts was harder, hence stories like that told by Abbot Robert of Newminster Abbey (Cistercian: Northumberland) who claimed to see the devil lurking outside the choir armed with his three-pronged fork ready to snatch monks who were not wholly focused on their religious duties.

From the twelfth century onwards the Choir area was equipped with hinged seats for the comfort of the monks during these services. Fourteenth-century examples survive at Chester Cathedral (formerly a Benedictine Abbey) and Winchester Cathedral (formerly served by an adjacent Benedictine Priory). When tilted these seats had a small projecting upper ledge upon which a monk could rest his bottom while standing upright during long religious services. Known as misericords (Latin: *misericordia*, mercy), the consoles of these load-bearing blocks or brackets provided ideal surfaces for carving. From at least the thirteenth century, they were often decorated with floral or religious subjects.

Apart from their regular choir duties, monks of every Order celebrated Mass (a sacred rite which sees the transubstantiation of bread and wine into Christ's body and blood) at least once a day, and twice on Sundays. There was also a weekly ritual of foot-washing known as Maunday, and special services on Feast days.

Another duty was to say prayers for the souls of the kings and members of the ruling elite whose patronage was the basis of monastic foundations and wealth. Many of these benefactors were buried in the main church and commemorated in heraldic wall paintings and stained-glass windows.

In addition to these daily rituals, the lives of monks were filled with religious ideas and thoughts ranging from the books they read, the sermons they heard, and the works of art they saw at every turn. These works included free-standing statues, architectural carvings such as roof bosses and capitals,

Tomb of John I (d. 1216) in the choir of Worcester Cathedral (Benedictine: Worcester), *c.* 1230.

Right:
Fourteenth-
century
stained-glass
panel from
a Tree of
Jesse scheme,
formerly at the
Cistercian Abbey
of Merevale,
now in the
parish church
of Our Lady,
Merevale,
(Warwickshire).

Top right:
Detail of mid-
thirteenth-century
wall painting
depicting St Faith,
Horsham St Faith
Priory
(Benedictine:
Norfolk), now a
private house.

Centre
Tiles depicting Eve
with the Apple at
Prior Crauden's
chapel, Ely
Cathedral Priory
(Benedictine: Ely,
Cambridgeshire),
c. 1324–5.

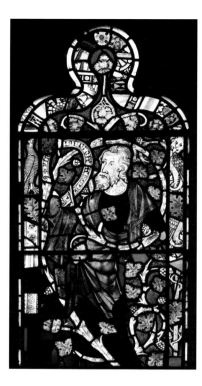

decorative tiles, stained-glass windows, vivid wall paintings, carved woodwork and beautifully painted altarpieces. For many, the impact of such imagery intensified their spiritual experiences. Although early Cistercian churches shunned such imagery, their monks had a particular affinity with the Virgin Mary, whose obedience to God had brought Christ into the world. Their churches were dedicated to her and her image appeared on their seals.

Monks also interacted with pilgrims who visited monasteries seeking cures or help from important miracle-working statues or relics. Such attractions were both prestigious and lucrative, with the gifts of pilgrims often funding ambitious new building programmes. At St Albans Abbey (Benedictine: Hertfordshire) the shrine of the eponymous Roman martyr

Painted panel
depicting Christ
at Binham Abbey
(Benedictine:
Norfolk), c. 1500,
overwritten after
the Reformation.

was guarded by a *custos feretri* (shrine-keeper) who kept vigil from a raised loft overlooking the tomb. At Canterbury Cathedral stained-glass windows depicted monks recording miracles at the shrine of Thomas Becket, the murdered archbishop, killed in 1170.

The Cure of Mad Matilda from Cologne, early thirteenth-century stained-glass window, Canterbury Cathedral (Benedictine priory: Kent).

Reconstructed shrine of St Alban with fifteenth-century watching loft, St Albans Abbey (Benedictine: now St Albans Cathedral).

Monks also showed important visitors around their abbeys. At Glastonbury (Benedictine: Somerset), manuscript leaves describing the history of the abbey were mounted in a wooden frame and hung on a pillar, much like a modern visitors' guide. Similar tables or *tableaux* are known to have been displayed at Hailes Abbey (Cistercian: Gloucestershire), and in other important abbey churches.

LECTIO DIVINA

According to one Carthusian monk, 'a monastery without books is like a kitchen without crockery'. Reading was an integral part of a monk's life and as late as the twelfth century monasteries were the largest storehouses of religious knowledge and ideas. Some had large libraries: in the thirteenth century Rievaulx Abbey had 212 volumes and by 1331 Canterbury Cathedral Priory already owned 1,831 books. Apart from service books and complete Bibles, typical libraries included individual books of the Bible for personal study (such as Judges and Kings from the Old Testament and Matthew and Mark from the New Testament, each with a marginal gloss or commentary written down the side of the page in a smaller script), various works of eminent theologians known as the Church Fathers (patristic books), as well as histories, hagiographies (lives of saints) and a smattering of classical texts.

Carrels in the south walk of Gloucester Abbey cloisters (Benedictine: now Gloucester Cathedral).

In the eleventh century, monks at Canterbury were given a new book to read every year. Spiritual growth through learning and scholarship was central to monastic culture. Monks sat behind one another in the cloister to prevent distractions or whispering and heads were uncovered so that none could pretend to be reading while sleeping. Monks were expected to read aloud, as silent reading was frowned upon.

The cloister alley nearest the church was often reserved for study, and carrels (desks) survive at Worcester Cathedral Priory (Benedictine: Worcestershire) and

Fourteenth-century book cupboard with elaborately carved tracery screen in the east cloister range at Valle Crucis Abbey (Cistercian: Denbighshire, Wales).

Gloucester Cathedral (formerly a Benedictine Abbey). Until the late Middle Ages most books were stored in a cupboard in the cloister, rather than in a separate room.

Many Cistercian monasteries marked their books with ownership inscriptions on the flyleaf. Some volumes were inscribed with curses on thieves or careless borrowers. At Reading Abbey (Cluniac: Berkshire) a mid-twelfth-century manuscript was given a fifteenth-century inscription threatening divine punishment against anyone who stole it from the monastery: *Liber sancte Marie Radying[ensis] quem qui alienaverit anathema sit.* ('This book belongs to St Mary's in Reading. A curse on whoever removes it.')

Sixteenth-century stained-glass panel, c. 1505–20, depicting Cistercian monks working in the fields, formerly in the cloisters of Altenberg Abbey (Cistercian: Germany) and now in the church of St Mary, Shrewsbury.

LABORA

St Benedict recognised that monks might become bored and jaded over time. To avoid disillusionment and restlessness, he believed that they needed to be kept busy, to vary their days and to occupy their minds with different tasks. While some assumed this meant that monks should help with household chores, by the tenth century wealthy monasteries, such as Cluny, were hiring servants to perform the majority of menial tasks. Peter the Venerable, Abbot from

Lay brothers' dormitory in the thirteenth-century Beaulieu Abbey (Cistercian: Hampshire).

The twelfth-century interior of Witham Friary, Lower church of Witham Charterhouse (Carthusian: Somerset).

1122 to 1156, was withering in his dismissal of the idea that educated monks should be 'begrimed in dirt and bent down with rustic labours'.

Early Cistercian abbeys, on the other hand, expected monks to undertake regular manual labour around their monasteries. This might involve gardening, painting and decorating, and helping at harvest time.

Even so, Cistercian monasteries also relied heavily on servants, especially a special (and segregated) category of lay brothers (*conversi*) who had their own quarters in the monastery and worshipped separately in the nave of the church. While such lay brothers mainly worked in the monastery precincts as cooks, brewers, beekeepers and porters, or as agricultural labourers in the outlying farms (granges), they also included skilled craftsmen and traders who represented the monastery at markets. At Buildwas Abbey (Cistercian: Shropshire) the monks were outnumbered by lay brothers by two to one; at late-twelfth-century Riveaulx there were about 140 monks and 500 lay brothers.

The system of lay brothers was already in decline before the great plague epidemics of the mid-fourteenth century; by the end of the century it had collapsed completely. At Meaux Abbey (Cistercian: Yorkshire) there had been ninety lay brothers in the mid-thirteenth century; after the Black Death (1348) there were none. By the time of the Dissolution, Cistercian monasteries relied entirely on paid servants.

Early Carthusian monasteries consisted of upper and lower sites with the monks living in the former and the lay brethren (*frères*) who undertook manual work, such as farming or chopping wood, residing in the lower site and worshipping in a separate church.

Part of a page for Easter Sunday from The Sherborne Missal with the monks John Whas and John Siferwas kneeling at the base of a column, 1399–1407.

Some monks produced books, working at desks and copying books from an exemplar of the same text. These had to be borrowed or acquired from elsewhere: Cistercian houses probably lent to one another; sometimes monks were sent from one abbey to another to make a copy of a book. Some twelfth-century books at Rochester Cathedral Priory were almost certainly borrowed from nearby Canterbury Cathedral Priory and copied not just word for word, but also in a distinctive 'prickly' script.

Between 1167 and 1173 the abbot of St Albans wrote several letters to the Prior of the monastery of St Victor in Paris asking if he could send a copyist to acquire texts written by one of the abbey's most admired theologians, Hugh of St Victor (*c*.1096–1141).

From the thirteenth century onwards, however, book production became more professional and many later manuscripts were written and painted by secular artists. An exception includes a beautiful Missal (book for the Mass) written and illustrated 1399–1407 by a monk at Sherborne Abbey (Benedictine: Dorset). It is signed: 'John Whas, the monk, this book's transcription undertaking, With early rising found his body aching'.

Interior of the fourteenth-century chapter house at Valle Crucis Abbey (Cistercian: Denbighshire, Wales).

Fragment of a wall painting with a scene from the Book of Revelation, *c.* 1360–70, Coventry Cathedral Priory chapter house (Benedictine: Coventry, Warwickshire), now in the care of the Priory Visitor Centre, Coventry.

CHAPTER-HOUSE MEETINGS

Apart from prayer, study and work, monks were also required to attend daily meetings in the chapter house. This was a large room off the east cloister alley which took its name from the portion or Chapter of the *Regula Benedicti* which was read from a lectern at the beginning of the proceedings. Such rooms could be highly decorative, with inlaid tiles and wall paintings. At Westminster Abbey (Benedictine: London) and Coventry Cathedral Priory (Benedictine: Warwickshire) the wall paintings depicted scenes from the biblical *Book of Revelation*, a text that Chapter XII of the *Regula Benedicti* required monks to learn by heart. During the meeting monks sat on stone benches which ran along the side walls, with the abbot or presiding officer occupying a higher seat in the centre of the east wall. At Westminster Abbey the monks were given mats to sit on. Meetings usually lasted less than an hour; topics included forthcoming services and events, administrative and business decisions including the sealing of documents, remembrance of the dead, and disciplinary matters within the community.

Chapter-house lectern, possibly made for Abbot Adam (1161–89) of Evesham Abbey (Benedictine: Worcestershire), now in the parish church of St Egwin, Norton and Lenchwick (Worcestershire).

DAILY LIFE II: PERSONAL LIFE

OBEDIENCE AND DISCIPLINE

Obedience and humility were cornerstones of monastic life. The subjugation of individual will to the *Regula* was paramount. From the outset St Benedict understood that if the same group of people were to live together for the whole of their lives, stability, discipline and consistency were essential. Hence breaches of the Rule were punished. Monks were expected to confess their sins at the daily chapter house meetings. Accusers were likened to 'the razor of God' who sought to remove 'unsightly hair' so that the penitent could become 'more pleasing'.

An artist's impression of a flogging in the chapter house.

Minor offences such as lateness, laziness or talking during silent periods were punished lightly and serious offences more sternly. Blasphemy, disruptive behaviour or rebellion could result in floggings, deportations to other monasteries, imprisonment or excommunication. At St Augustine's Abbey, Canterbury (Benedictine: Kent) the customary advised monks to 'sit with bowed and covered heads and … have compassion' if one of their brethren was flogged. When the ruins of Fountains Abbey were excavated in the nineteenth century, several cells were discovered below the abbot's house, each with an iron staple in the floor for attaching a prisoner's chains. One cell had the words *vale libertas* (farewell, liberty) scratched in the wall. In the late middle ages, punishments were less harsh, with errant monks typically excluded from the company of others rather than being beaten.

Detail of *Warning to Swearers*, a fifteenth-century wall painting in the parish church of St Lawrence, Broughton, Buckinghamshire. A swearer holds a foot, which his blasphemy has torn from Christ's body.

Some monasteries were less strict than others; newly appointed abbots and visitations by Bishops often discovered lapses. In the early fourteenth century monks at St Albans Abbey were told not to swear by the wounds, blood or limbs of Christ — a common blasphemy rebuked in contemporary wall paintings.

A hundred years later not much had changed: their successors were exhorted to be punctual at Vespers; not to leave the quire during a service in order to walk about the church and talk; not to loiter and chatter at the vestry door; not to swear nor address each other discourteously; and not to go to a nearby nunnery without permission.

Inevitably some monks ran away. Perhaps the tedium was too much; possibly their religious ardour waned; maybe they fell out with the abbey authorities. Such an offence was called 'apostasy' and the offenders were usually pursued. Only very rarely was a woman involved. The Records of Eynsham Abbey for 1445 mention a monk who had absconded with a nun from nearby Godstow Priory (Benedictine: Oxfordshire), but who had been brought back to the monastery and was doing penance. An incident with a less happy ending occurred at Rievaulx Abbey in 1279 when a restless monk, William de Aketon, tried to hoodwink the abbot into letting him leave by claiming that he had contracted leprosy and thus posed a health risk to the others. After a suspicious obedientiary demanded to examine him, William drew a knife and stabbed his interrogator before fleeing into the woods. When he was caught shortly afterwards he was savagely beaten and died a few days later in the monastery.

POVERTY AND CLOTHING

Although poverty was another key vow taken by professed monks, it rarely meant that they lived like genuinely poor people. On the contrary, many monks had a relatively high standard of living compared to the wider population, with diets, accommodation and sanitation far better than average. From the thirteenth century Benedictine monks often received wages; at Peterborough Abbey (Benedictine: Cambridgeshire, now Peterborough Cathedral) they received £25 a year.

A better interpretation of the vow is that monks eschewed personal possessions. Thus a monk's clothes and bedding belonged to the community, not to the wearer, and monks were not supposed to own their furniture.

The clothing consisted of two tunics (habits) and two cloak/hoods (cowls) together with an apron-like garment known as a *scapula* which was worn for work. Shoes, stockings and a belt were also issued. St Benedict's rules about clothing had been written for monks in southern Europe; additions allowed for the harsher winters in Britain included trousers, caps and woolly socks. Carthusian monks habitually wore a scratchy hair shirt below their habit to remind them of humility and to curb sensual pleasures.

Novice monks were taught how to wear their habits: not to let them drag along the ground; not to let others see them naked; how to avoid eye contact by keeping their hoods up while using the latrines; not to leave their clothes in a mess.

CHASTITY

Sexual chastity was another of the defining vows of a monk. Self-control and denial was reinforced by stories and images, rules and regulations. The experiences of holy men were held up as examples to the young. At Worcester Cathedral Priory the cloister glazing included scenes from the early life of St Wulfstan (*c.* 1008–95), the last Anglo-Saxon Bishop in England, who

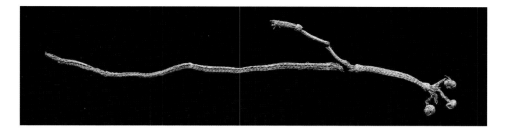

reputedly jumped in a bramble bush to quell his lust when an attractive young woman attempted to make 'a shipwreck of his chastity'. At the parish church of St Leonard at Marston Bigot (Somerset) a panel of sixteenth-century glass displaced from the cloisters of a German Cistercian abbey depicts St Bernard of Clairvaux in bed shouting *'Fures, fures'* [Latin: 'thieves'] after a promiscuous innkeeper's wife had tried to 'steal his chastity'. A ban on eating red meat was another way that monks imagined physical desires could be curbed, and some monks may have resorted to self-flagellation to suppress their sensuality. Misogamy was rife, and a flirtatious woman was to be feared as a reincarnated 'Eve', whose temptations could lead to spiritual disaster. Homosexuality was a serious offence and senior monks patrolled the dormitory and latrines at night to prevent any possible misbehaviour.

Plaited metal scourge excavated at Rievaulx Abbey (Cistercian: Yorkshire).

Cases of sexual immorality were fewer than is often presumed. Between 1347 and 1540, for example, only fifteen cases of sexual impropriety were recorded in the numerous religious houses of Yorkshire.

FRIENDS AND ENEMIES

St Benedict said next to nothing about friendship. In the modern sense of the word it was probably assumed to be part of the world that monks had chosen to leave behind. While monastic authors extolled the ideas of communal friendship (*amicitia*) as a way of reaching God, private friendships may have been regarded as incompatible with these ideals. Even so, surviving letters between some monks hint at personal emotional bonds. The wills of two former monks at St Albans Abbey, who died in 1540 and 1545 respectively, requested burial side by side.

Just as friendships could bloom, so too could dislikes, factionalism and conflict. In 1394 the monks at Hailes Abbey were told to stop reviling one another; in 1433 a monk at Combe Abbey (Cistercian: Warwickshire) fled to Waverley Abbey (Cistercian: Surrey) blaming 'the malice of his rivals'; when Bishop Richard Nix (alternative spellings include Nyx, or Nykke) visited Wymondham Priory (Benedictine: Norfolk) in 1514 he was told that the prior had suffered a breakdown, attacking some of the monks with a stone and drawing a sword on another.

DAILY LIFE III: DOMESTIC

FOOD AND DRINK

Meals were mainly eaten in the refectory, usually a two-storied hall off the cloisters; some of these halls were extremely large. At Worcester Cathedral Priory the refectory still survives as part of an adjoining school. It is 120 feet long and 32 feet wide with an over-sized carving of an enthroned Christ in Majesty on the east wall. At Rievaulx Abbey the ruined hall is 126 feet long and 80 feet high.

At Cleeve Abbey (Cistercian: Somerset) the refectory was remodelled in the fifteenth century and given a timber roof adorned with carved bosses and angels while a wall painting of the Crucifixion (now lost) filled the east wall. At Dover Priory (Benedictine: Kent) a wall painting (also lost) depicting the Last Supper before Christ's crucifixion provided 'food for thought' as the monks ate.

Before entering the *frater* monks washed their hands in a *lavatorium*, either a long trough built into the cloister wall (as at Gloucester and Worcester) or a free-standing covered structure in the cloister garth containing a basin set on a circular or polygonal base as at Wenlock Priory(Cluniac: Shropshire). In both cases the lavers were supplied with piped water and drains. Such lavers could be lavishly decorated. At Gloucester Abbey the ceiling of the laver was enriched with fan vaulting; at Wenlock Priory the base of the trough included carved panels, one of which showed Christ calling the Apostles on the Sea of Galilee. Fresh towels were stored in nearby cupboards.

Spoons and napkins were collected as the monks entered the refectory. There was a raised dais or platform at the end furthest from the entrance where the abbot and his senior officers presided and benches along the side walls where the monks sat, facing inwards.

Benches and tables could be free-standing or set on stone legs. At Bardney Abbey (Benedictine: Lincolnshire) the wooden table tops were about 20 feet long and rested on Y-shaped stone supports carved with the heads of a monk, abbot and king on the visible side. The wall benches had similar supports.

Former refectory (1330s), Worcester Cathedral Priory, now part of the adjacent King's School.

41

Right: The stairs leading to Cleeve Abbey refectory (Cistercian: Somerset), which dates from the fifteenth century.

Far right: Fan-vaulted laver in north cloister wall, fifteenth-century, Gloucester Abbey (Benedictine: now Gloucester Cathedral).

Below: Artist's impression of Cleeve Abbey refectory.

Every meal began with Grace, a prayer of thanks. During the meal a senior monk read aloud from a pulpit-style lectern built into the wall or a window splay. Good examples survive in the parish church at Beaulieu (see page 44), formerly the refectory of Beaulieu Abbey (Cistercian: Hampshire), and at Chester Cathedral (formerly a Benedictine abbey). Anybody who spilt his drink or otherwise interrupted the reader had to stand up and lie prostrate on the floor until told to return to his place. At Sawley Abbey (Cistercian: Lancashire) novices who finished their meals before others were advised to occupy their time by arranging the bread-crumbs on the tablecloth into the form of a cross.

Christ calling Peter and Andrew on the Sea of Galilee, thirteenth-century laver panel at Wenlock Priory (Cluniac: Shropshire).

In the early Middle Ages a typical meal lasted about half an hour and was served once a day in the winter and twice in the summer when days were longer. Monks were expected to eat quietly and cleanly. Wiping hands, mouths and knives on tablecloths was prohibited. Talking was forbidden although sign language (see page 53) was permitted. Benedictines usually ate better than the early Cistercians, who regarded food as a necessity rather than a pleasurable treat. Some monks fasted excessively and ate very little. In the early twelfth century a typical monastic diet consisted of cereals or

Artist's impression of the Wenlock Priory laver.

43

cooked vegetables (*pulmenta*), enriched with small portions of protein such as egg, cheese or fish. Home-grown fruit might also be offered. It seems that sometimes the cuisine was stomach-churning – a twelfth-century monk at Rievaulx Abbey complained that the food was 'more bitter than wormwood' – but in general, portions were adequate as under-nourishment would have been pointless. In addition to the basic dishes, each monk also received a daily allowance of bread and a measure of ale. On special occasions, such as saints' days or the anniversary of the monastery's foundation, this diet was augmented by additional or better-quality dishes, known as 'pittances'.

Flavouring was limited to salt or vinegars in case richly flavoured foods induced sluggishness and distracted monks from prayer and work.

Although red meat was never served in the refectory, monks were not vegetarians in the modern sense. The origins of the ban lay in fears that eating meat would arouse sexual and other physical desires and temptations. As a result meat was initially only served in the infirmary where it was thought to assist a patient's recovery, but these rules were gradually relaxed during the later Middle Ages. From the late twelfth century onwards Benedictine and Cluniac monks were eating meat in a special chamber, known as a *misericord* ('mercy') with Cistercians following suit in the early fourteenth century. Once again the Carthusians were different, refusing to eat meat under any circumstances, including serving it to the sick, in case its pleasures tempted monks to feign illnesses!

Lectern in the former refectory of Beaulieu Abbey, now Beaulieu Abbey Church (Cistercian: Hampshire).

In line with rising prosperity and changes in monastic practices, by the late Middle Ages the diets of most monks had improved dramatically. Even allowing for the fact that wealthy monasteries often entertained important guests, a single week's kitchen bill at Dover Priory in 1530 reads like a feast. It included payments for mutton, lamb, geese and capons, oysters, salt salmon, fresh fish, butter and eggs.

Based on the early sixteenth-century account rolls at Westminster Abbey it has been estimated that each monk consumed an average of two pounds of meat or fish each day, one gallon of ale, and a loaf of bread weighing two and a half pounds. Stews and cheese flans were popular while only small amounts of fruit and vegetables were eaten. Some Cistercian abbeys were little different: in 1520 two thirds of Whalley Abbey's (Lancashire) income – £640 out of a total of £895 – was spent on food and drink, including dates, figs and sugar. Studies of skeletons recovered from the cemeteries of Stratford Langthorne Abbey (Cistercian: London) and Bermondsey Abbey (Cluniac: London) show evidence of diffuse idiopathic skeletal hyperostosis (DISH), a condition associated with a calorie-rich diet and obesity (with attendant late-onset diabetes).

Diets were much richer in wealthy sixteenth-century monasteries.

SLEEP

With the exception of Carthusians, who lived alone in their individual cells, most monks slept communally in a long, unheated first-floor dormitory. The beds had straw mattresses and were ranged along the walls with storage cupboards and chests lining the centre of the room. Towards the end of the Middle Ages many monasteries fitted partitions between the beds to give

monks a greater degree of privacy. Apart from the entrance from the cloister ('day stairs') some dormitories also included stairs leading directly into the church for night-time services; these were known as the 'night stairs'.

Fifteenth-century oak chest at Pershore Abbey (Benedictine: Worcestershire).

Sleep proved difficult for many as they were woken up during the middle of the night by bells or roused by others to proceed to the church to sing the Night Office. Lateness was a disciplinary offence, as was falling asleep during services; senior monks would shine lights in the faces of any monks who seemed drowsy.

A combination of interrupted sleep, together with other disturbances, such as the unsettling sounds of snoring and the cries of monks suffering nightmares or ecstatic visions, caused various sleeping disorders, including insomnia. When monks at Sawley Abbey complained of difficulties in getting to sleep they were told to imagine their beds were their graves; at Forde Abbey (Cistercian: Dorset) monks prayed over the bed of an insomniac until he was cured.

Dormitories were also patrolled by senior monks to monitor behaviour and to ensure that candles were extinguished. Talking was forbidden. As monks slept in their habits, other rules stipulated that even in the heat of

Opposite:
The night stairs, Hexham Abbey (Augustinian: Northumberland).

Below: The fifteenth-century dormitory at Cleeve Abbey (Cistercian: Somerset).

summer only their heads, feet and arms could be exposed in case demons were drawn to their bare flesh.

In early monasteries abbots slept in the same dormitory as other monks but as institutions become more prosperous many lived in luxurious lodgings either in the claustral range or in separate houses. At Fountains Abbey the infirmary hall was remodelled in the fifteenth century to create self-contained two-storey apartments for senior monks.

LATRINES

The dormitory also included an entrance to the first-floor latrine block. Cubicles were separated by screens. At Lewes Priory (Cluniac: East Sussex) there were

Artist's impression of latrines.

The Abbot's parlour at fifteenth-century Muchelney Abbey (Benedictine: Somerset).

at least fifty-nine cubicles for a population of about one hundred monks. There was also an enclosed room which may have been used as a bathhouse.

As the workings of the 'lower body', particularly excrement (material corruption) were often seen as the embodiment of sin, latrines were feared as the haunt of demons that wallowed in the filth and stink of the dropslots. According to a history of St Albans Abbey written about 1390, an untrustworthy twelfth-century monk named William Pygun died in the latrines after the other monks heard a voice rising from the dungpit urging Satan to seize him.

Because of restrictions on the times and conditions for visiting the latrines monks made use of portable urinals known as 'jordans' whose contents were subsequently used for bleaching cloth or tanning animal skins. Drains often flushed into ditches, rivers, soakaways, and sometimes even fishponds where the excreta nourished the plankton on which the fish fed. At Muchelney Abbey (Benedictine: Somerset) the latrine block retains a series of arches at ground-floor level, which were the outflow to a sewer.

HEALTH AND SICKNESS

As noted earlier, monks had a relatively high standard of living compared to the general population, with diets and sanitation better than average. In the fifteenth century, applicants to the Benedictine Order were screened and asked if they had any contagious diseases. Infirmary accounts seldom name specific ailments, but in the sixteenth century some monks at Westminster Abbey were listed as suffering from a complaint known as 'morbus in tibia', a disease of the shinbone – possibly leg ulcers caused by a lack of vitamin C in their diet. Excavations on the infirmary site at Beaulieu Abbey unearthed a number of skeletons of men aged over sixty who were crippled by chronic rheumatism.

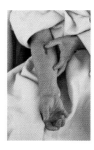

Monks were bled up to nine times a year.

Contemporary medical opinion believed that regular bloodletting, otherwise known as 'seyney' (from the French *seigné*: 'bled'), was an important contribution to maintaining good health and repressing sexual temptation. Some monks were bled nine times a year, usually in the warming room or the infirmary, a separate complex lying outside the cloister enclosure equipped with its own chapel, cloister, refectory, dorter, latrine and kitchens. This block also often accommodated elderly and infirm members of the community.

Such bloodletting sessions may have been enjoyed by some monks, as meat was served afterwards to assist their recovery. As part of the same 'treat' they were often allowed to stay overnight in the warmer and quieter confines of the infirmary or convalesce at a country property.

Infirmaries could be large with lofty roofs and a fireplace at one end of the hall or ward. At Ely Cathedral Priory (Benedictine: Cambridgeshire) the infirmary was a 192-foot-long rectangular building with side aisles. After the Dissolution the side-aisle arches were blocked up and the roofless central

Firmary Lane, Ely Cathedral Priory (Benedictine: Cambridgeshire).

floor space converted to a road now known as Firmary Lane. Infirmaries elsewhere were almost as large: at Fountains Abbey the infirmary hall measured 180 feet by 78 feet; at Furness Abbey (Cistercian: Cumbria) it stretched to 125 feet by 50 feet.

Infirmaries were manned by specially trained staff. Physicians, surgeons and apothecaries were usually hired as required, although among the letters of the future Edward II is a request to the Abbot of Reading Abbey in 1302–3 asking if the monks could care for one of his friends who had wounded his hand, as he understood they 'had a good surgeon at the house'.

At Norwich Cathedral Priory (Benedictine: Norfolk) the infirmary had its own garden where herbs and medicinal plants were grown, such as rhubarb, peonies (the roots, flowers, and seeds were all used in the medieval pharmacy), fennel, and squills. Infusions of catmint, parsley, lovage, celery, pennyroyal, wild thyme and fennel were used to combat colds. Surviving accounts of this wealthy monastery show that liquorice, aniseed, and dragon's blood (a resin from certain trees and shrubs that was used to treat diarrhoea, dysentery diseases and other illnesses), were among the more exotic drugs and spices purchased for the benefit of the monks. Gifts of medicine to the poor are also recorded.

An artist's impression of the infirmary.

SIGN LANGUAGE

Some signs were based on miming actions. The Ely sign book includes:

- For a book, extend the hand and move it as the page of a book is usually turned
- For bread, make a circle with both thumbs and the next two fingers
- For a ration of wine, turn the hollowed hand downwards
- For honey, put out the tongue and touch it with fingers as if you wish to lick

- For a knife, draw the hand across the middle of the palm
- For sleep, place hands on cheek as when sleeping
- For silence, place a finger on closed mouth
- For saying 'no', place the tip of the middle finger under the thumb and make it spring back as with a flick
- For something good, place the thumb on one cheek and other fingers on the other and draw gently downwards onto the chin.

The sign for bread

The sign for a ration of wine

The sign for honey

The sign for a knife

The sign for silence

The sign for sleep

SILENCE

Although monasteries were intended to be oases of contemplation and peace, their calmness was frequently jarred by the pattering of servants, builders and visitors. Monks themselves, however, were prohibited from talking during church services, in the dormitory at night, and during mealtimes in the refectory. Where conversations were permitted in the cloisters or parlours, they were expected to be brief and businesslike. Gossiping was frowned upon as frivolous and potentially dangerous, either because it could foment tensions and jealousies within the community or because it could lead to dissent and disobedience to the abbot and the senior office holders.

During the ninth century the monks at Cluny Abbey developed a sophisticated sign language to circumvent these prohibitions, which was subsequently written down and learned by novice monks. The earliest written Anglo-Saxon sign list to survive in England – the *Monasteriales Indiciae*, containing 127 signs – was probably compiled in the late tenth century and copied into a manuscript used by monks at Canterbury Cathedral Priory in the mid-eleventh century. Two fourteenth-century lists from Bury St Edmunds Abbey contain 141 and 198 signs respectively. Around 1500 the monks at Ely Cathedral Priory used a list of 109 signs.

Most sign lists consisted of simple nouns, adjectives and a few verbs. They include signs relevant to church services, eating and drinking in the refectory, and discussing everyday activities in the cloister. In some eyes even this was too many. When the Welsh historian, Gerald of Wales (1146–*c*.1223), ate at Canterbury Cathedral Priory in 1180 he complained, 'There were the monks ... all of them gesticulating with fingers, hands and arms and whistling to one another instead of speaking ... so that I seemed to be seated at a stage play or among actors and jesters.'

ENTERTAINMENT

Although primarily 'houses of prayer' and reverence, monks also laughed and played. They were neither unworldly nor meek; sobriety was interspersed with moments of warmth ... and occasional profanity. Despite the disapproval of senior church figures, for much of the Middle Ages Benedictine monasteries often elected a 'boy abbot' in December, signalling several days of feasting and play with novices changing places with the superior of the house. Entertainers were also hired by wealthy houses: at

Board game, north cloister walk, Gloucester Abbey (Benedictine: now Gloucester Cathedral).

Durham Cathedral Priory the accounts book includes numerous entries for the costs of musicians and players, including twelve minstrels at the Feast of Saint Cuthbert in 1375–6. At Boxgrove (Benedictine: Sussex) the prior was admonished in 1518 for entering into archery matches with lay people, while at Chester Abbey the monks were chided by a visiting Bishop in 1315 and 1323 for feeding the leftovers from the refectory to their greyhounds rather than giving them to the poor. Dice, cards, and games such as 'Nine Men's Morris'

The incised grave-slab of William Alford (d. 1490), Abbot of Bordesley Abbey (Cistercian: Worcestershire) now stands in the parish church of St Peter, Hinton on the Green (Worcestershire).

and 'Fox and Geese' were also played; a stone bench in the cloisters of Gloucester Cathedral retains a scratched board for playing the latter game. Allegations of late-night drinking sessions blighted some monasteries. When the diarist Margery Kempe (1378–c.1438) visited Hailes Abbey in 1417, she was shocked by monks who swore crude oaths in her presence. On a lighter note, in the sixteenth century, monks from Durham took it in turns to enjoy short 'holidays' at Finchale priory (Benedictine: Co. Durham), four miles north of the city. Even the Carthusians relaxed with a weekly socialising walk, the *spatiamentum*. In every sense monks remained very human.

DYING

In most monasteries death was an elaborate ritual. At Syon Abbey (Bridgettine: Middlesex), a fashionable nunnery on the western outskirts of London, an open grave was maintained near the entrance to the church to remind worshippers that death was inevitable and judgement certain. At Canterbury Cathedral Priory when a monk was close to death the entire community gathered in the church and processed to the infirmary where the dying man was sprinkled with holy water ('asperged') and made a public confession of his sins. Cistercians deputed rotas of monks to sit with their dying colleagues.

After death, Benedictine and Cistercian monks were laid out on the ground on a sackcloth which had been placed on a cross-shaped scatter of ashes. Their bodies were thereafter washed, wrapped in a shroud and buried without a coffin in the monastic cemetery. Carthusian monks were buried in the cloister garth.

Cluniacs were laid on a hair shirt and hooded habit, with their hands arranged as if in prayer. Abbots were often buried in chapter houses together with their regalia of office, such as their rings and crozier (a staff with a head shaped like a shepherd's crook). At Bury St Edmunds Abbey two abbots were laid before an image of the Virgin Mary at the north entrance to the choir. At St Augustine's Abbey at Canterbury, Abbot Roger II (d. 1272) was interred in a coffin with a stone pillow for his head.

In many monasteries gifts were made to the poor in memory of the dead monk. At Evesham Abbey (Benedictine: Worcestershire) this included a 'seam' of corn (a seam was worth eight bushels, one bushel being equivalent to eight gallons).

The grave of Abbot Roger II (1252–72) was excavated in 1918 from the south transept of St Augustine's Abbey church (Benedictine: Canterbury, Kent). Note the stone pillow beneath his head.

BEYOND THE CLOISTER

DESPITE LIVING APART, monks were not entirely cut off from the outside world. Many visited local towns or other abbeys and some went on pilgrimage. Others played a wider role within the church, such as when the Carthusian monk, Hugh of Avalon (*c.* 1135–1200), became Bishop of Lincoln in 1186, or the sacrist of Bury St Edmunds was elected Abbot of Thorney Abbey in 1217 (Benedictine: Cambridgeshire). At a personal level, while the Carthusians forbade monks from leaving their monasteries for home visits, the other Orders were not as rigid. Thirteenth-century monks at St Albans Abbey were permitted 'home visits' to see sick or dying relatives, but only for short periods and if accompanied by a colleague. Towards the end of the Middle Ages, however, these rules were relaxed further and monks were also allowed to pay social visits to their families and friends.

Conversely, visits from family members were tolerated. At Beaulieu Abbey a monk's family was permitted to visit once or twice a year and to stay two nights on each occasion. There were similar arrangements at Abingdon Abbey (Benedictine: formerly Berkshire, now Oxfordshire). In the early fifteenth century the cellarer at Westminster Abbey allocated 200 gallons of ale each year for family visits.

Even if they had wished to, monks could not avoid the problems that flared outside their walled enclosures. Some abbeys in the north of England were damaged during wars between England and Scotland, while in Wales the crops and estates of several Cistercian monasteries, including Valle Crucis (Denbighshire, Wales), suffered during the Welsh wars of Edward I, eventually receiving reparation payments from the crown. Later still the abbeys of St Albans and Stratford Langthorne were among those vandalised during the Peasants' Revolt of 1381.

Monks in larger monasteries also kept in touch with political affairs as important visitors came and went. Matthew Paris (*c.* 1200–59), a thirteenth-century monk at St Albans Abbey, corresponded with important people during the writing of his *History of England* and had long conversations with Henry III, while John Stone, a monk at Canterbury Cathedral Priory between 1417 and 1472, kept a chronicle in which he recorded that he saw a camel when the patriarch of Antioch visited the city in 1466.

Some Benedictine cathedral priories maintained their own colleges at Oxford University to which monks were sent. In 1437, a college for Cistercian monks was also founded in the same city. After the Dissolution, some of these college sites were reconstituted under different names; thus Durham Cathedral College (Benedictine) became Trinity College and St Bernard's College (Cistercian) became St John's.

Abbots of richer monasteries also played important roles at court and a few were summoned to medieval parliaments.

Local disputes such as clashes with tenants are recorded, with riots at Bury St Edmunds in 1327 which saw the abbot kidnapped; there was also an extraordinary event at Colchester Abbey (Benedictine: Essex) in 1272 when monks removed the body of a thief from the gallows and attempted to persuade the coroner that it was the corpse of an innocent man who had been slain by townspeople during a fight with abbey servants during the Midsummer fair.

The fifteenth-century gatehouse of Abingdon Abbey (Benedictine, Oxfordshire).

Sometimes trouble broke into the cloisters. In the fourteenth century a thief was caught after sneaking into the infirmary at Chertsey Abbey (Benedictine: Surrey) – during the ensuing struggle one of the monks, who was also a priest, climbed out of his sick-bed, seized a sword and struck the robber who subsequently died. An investigation cleared him of any wrongdoings after it was decided that the intruder had probably died as a result of wounds inflicted by servants who had also joined the fight.

Natural disasters were never far away: many monasteries suffered from flooding and famines, and from the fourteenth century onwards plague epidemics were a recurring fear. At Meaux Abbey, for example, the abbot and twenty-two monks died within a few weeks of one another in August 1349 as the 'Black Death' swept northwards.

NUNNERIES

R ELIGIOUSLY DEVOUT WOMEN who embraced the monastic life were known as nuns (from the Latin *nonna*, the feminine of *nonnus*, 'monk'). Those who joined Anglo-Saxon nunneries, such as at Whitby (Yorkshire) and Wilton (Wiltshire), were the daughters, sisters or widows of the wealthy elite, but by the fifteenth century the majority of nuns seem to have been drawn from local gentry families. As in male monasteries, nuns' lives revolved around set hours of communal prayer, and periods of reading and recreation. Yet despite sharing many of these same routines, there were also important differences between nunneries and male monasteries.

First, there were far fewer nunneries than male houses; probably around one-sixth as many. Estimates vary but some suggest that at the peak of monasticism in England in the thirteenth century, the total number of nuns was only about 2,500. At the Dissolution these numbers had fallen to perhaps 1,500, living in about seventy Benedictine nunneries, thirty loosely defined Cistercian houses and one Cluniac convent. The Carthusians never admitted women and the Cistercians formally recognised only two of the nunneries that affiliated themselves with their Order, the abbeys of Tarrant (Dorset) and Marham (Norfolk).

Next, with a few exceptions, most nunneries were also smaller and poorer than their male equivalents. Because women were barred from the priesthood and were not ordained to conduct masses on behalf of the dead or perform other sacraments of the church, they had less appeal to wealthy donors than their male counterparts. Even so, the sixteenth-century nuns at Redlingfield Priory (Benedictine: Suffolk) had individual bedrooms with feather pillows, and a church with alabaster carvings known as 'tables' and a silver pyx and chalices on their altar.

An interesting feature of nunneries is that about a third had their cloisters on the north side of the church; male monasteries were usually built on the south side. One suggestion is that it replicated the segregation of the sexes in churches and reflected Mary's position on the right-hand side of Christ at the Crucifixion. Other significant differences concerned entry, enclosure, and spirituality.

The canonical age at which a woman could 'profess' her vows was sixteen, and most novices seem to have entered a convent between fifteen and seventeen years of age, although some older women also entered monasteries, perhaps after their husbands had abandoned them, or as widows. Novices were expected to bring their own bedding with them as well as a £5 dowry before undergoing a year-long trial during which they studied the psalms, antiphons and responses of the Canonical Hours or Offices. Entrants were expected to

An early sixteenth-century panel painting of an abbess, Romsey Abbey (Benedictine nunnery: Hampshire).

be legitimately born (of a marriage) and to have knowledge of, or an ability to learn, Latin. At the nunnery of St George at Thetford (Benedictine: Norfolk) in 1492, fears were raised that the prioress might admit 'unlearned and even deformed persons'. Occasionally there were allegations that women had been forced to enter nunneries against their will. The admission ceremony was presided over by the Bishop and held in the monastic church with a more elaborate ritual for virgins than women who had been married. Unlike monks, whose heads were shaved (tonsured), a nun's hair was shorn. Instead of a habit

Alabaster 'table' depicting the Ascension of the Virgin Mary, c. 1480 (private collection).

and cowl, they wore a habit or cloak with a wimple and veil. Benedictine nuns wore black habits; 'Cistercian' nuns wore white.

The organisation of nunneries was similar to those of monasteries, with an abbess (or prioress) as the superior officer who had to be obeyed. Male chaplains and servants were also ruled by the abbess. Typical punishments for errant nuns included fasting, saying penitential psalms and losing rank in the choir. In 1516–17 it was reported that some of the nuns at Littlemore Priory (Benedictine: Oxford) had rescued another who had been imprisoned in stocks by the prioress. In 1535 a nun at Esholt Priory (Cistercian: Yorkshire) who became pregnant was sentenced to two years' imprisonment in a room within the nuns' dormitory.

By far the most important difference between male and female monasteries, however, were the efforts of church authorities to force nuns to lead fully enclosed lives. Such ordinances were not part of St Benedict's original rules and

Late fifteenth-century stained- glass panel depicting a Cistercian abbess/nun/patron of Llanllugan Abbey (Cistercian nunnery: Powys, Wales). The glass is now in the parish church of St Mary at Llanllugan.

were officially promulgated in a decree issued by Pope Boniface VIII in 1298, known as *Periculoso*. These edicts attempted to restrict women from leaving their cloisters except in the case of a parent dying and then for only a limited period of time.

Recent studies have suggested that the relative poverty and low status of most nunneries combined with the physical isolation caused by enclosure fostered a distinct female spirituality, with women embracing their poverty as an active ideal and forging lives distinguished by a quiet and dignified piety. Although there are exceptions to this generalisation, with some nuns growing their hair longer and wearing silver pins in their wimples, it does seem that that their alms-giving was higher than equivalent male houses and their reputations and standing in local communities correspondingly better.

THE OTHER ORDERS

IN ADDITION TO THE FOUR MAIN ORDERS, a number of diverse quasi-monastic orders proliferated from the eleventh century onwards, providing opportunities for patrons to endow a new wave of monasteries. Known as Canons Regular, these orders consisted of priests who lived together in abbeys and priories while at the same time undertaking pastoral duties in the outside world. Unlike those who followed the *Regula Benedicti*, they based their lives on a series of short letters written by a fifth-century Bishop of Hippo (now Annaba, Algeria), usually known as the 'Rule of St Augustine' (*Regula Sancti Augustini*). Rather than providing a detailed handbook of communal life, these treatises focused on the spiritual life of the community and were less severe than for those in monastic orders. The Augustinians arrived in England in *c.* 1106 and at the height of their appeal had over two hundred houses, including fifteen nunneries. The present-day cathedrals of Bristol, Oxford, Portsmouth and Southwark were originally Augustinian foundations; nunneries included Lacock (Wiltshire). Their first house in Wales was at Llanthony in the Black Mountains. While many canons were active in parish churches and founded hospitals such as St Thomas and St Bartholomew in London, a few imitated the monastic life and had hardly any pastoral contact with lay people.

A related variant from this Order was the Arrouaisian Order of Augustine Canons, so-called after the Abbey of Arrouaise in northern France where it was founded in the 1130s. As admirers of the Cistercians, they wore white instead of the black of most Augustinians. They founded Dorchester Abbey (Oxfordshire), Lilleshall Abbey (Staffordshire), and a priory in Carlisle which was given cathedral status in 1133.

Another offshoot was the Trinitarian Canons for the Redemption of Captives, who raised money to pay ransoms for Christians kidnapped by pirates. They had twelve houses in England, all small.

The second most important and numerous of the groups of Canons Regular, the Premonstratensian or Norbertine canons, were the creation of St Norbert of Xanten (*c.* 1080–1134), of the Abbey of Prémontré,

Opposite: Chapter-house entrance with statues of St Katherine of Alexandria (*left*) and St John the Evangelist (*right*) at Haughmond Abbey (Augustinian: Shropshire). The arches date from the twelfth century; the statues from the fourteenth century.

near Laon, 75 miles east of Paris. Norbert was a friend of Bernard of Clairvaux and his Order combined Augustinian rule with some of the characteristics of the Cistercians. The Premonstratensians arrived in England in 1130 and eventually established thirty-one abbeys, including Shap (Cumbria), Torre (Devon), Titchfield (Hampshire), and Halesowen (West Midlands).

Yet another order, the Gilbertines, was the only religious order exclusive to England. The origin of the order lay in the founder's desire to provide double houses for canons and nuns. St Gilbert's first house was at Sempringham (Lincolnshire); the second at Haverholme, near Sleaford (Lincolnshire). He was also a great admirer of the Cistercians and wanted to cede his communities to that Order but the French declined to admit the Lincolnshire women. Nine double monasteries and four houses of canons were founded in his lifetime. After his death in 1189 only two more nunneries were founded and the remaining foundations were restricted to canons only.

In 1415 Henry V endowed Syon Abbey at Isleworth (Middlesex), a monastery for nuns of the Bridgettine Order, an offshoot from the Augustinians founded in Sweden in 1350.

There were also several Military Orders – the Knights Templar and the Knights Hospitallers – who maintained 'preceptories' or 'commanderies' (church and living quarters) in Britain while concentrating their efforts in the Middle East.

Although not monks, another important religious group of people who shared communal lives were the mendicant friars, who depended on charitable gifts and devoted their lives to preaching. Although friaries followed the usual monastic plan, with a large church and a range of buildings arranged around a central cloister, including a refectory and dormitory, their inhabitants were active in local communities. The first friars to arrive were the French Dominicans ('black friars') in 1221. Thereafter Italian Franciscans ('grey friars') landed in 1224, followed by the Carmelites ('white friars') in 1242. The Austin (Augustinian) Friars also reached England in the 1240s. By the 1530s there were fifty-three houses of Dominicans in England, sixty houses of Franciscans, thirty-seven houses of Carmelites, and thirty-four houses of Austin Friars. There was also one priory of Dominican nuns and three of Franciscan nuns. The latter are sometimes called Minoresses, as female members of the Order of Friars Minor, the official name of the Franciscan Order founded by St Francis of Assisi (*c.* 1181/2–1226), or 'Poor Clares', officially the Order of Saint Clare, an exclusively female order founded by St Clare of Assisi (1194–1253), a follower of St Francis.

Opposite:
Canopy of the shrine of St Edbergh (*c.* 1294–1317), from Bicester Priory (Augustinian: Oxfordshire), now in the parish church of St Michael, Stanton Harcourt (Oxfordshire).

DISSOLUTION

THE SUPPRESSION OF MONASTICISM would have seemed inconceivable at the beginning of the sixteenth century. Although the number of monks had shrunk since the high peaks of the twelfth and thirteenth centuries, most of the larger abbeys were financially stable, books were being bought and major building programmes were still being commissioned. The Carthusian priory at Mount Grace (Yorkshire) even had a waiting list of people wanting to join. But when the end came it was sudden and unstoppable.

The indirect cause of the destruction was the Pope's refusal to grant Henry VIII a divorce from Catherine of Aragon (1485–1536), which he needed in order to marry Anne Boleyn (1501–36). Determined to press ahead without papal approval, the king declared himself Supreme Head of the English Church in 1534 and aligned himself with the Protestant Reformation, triggering a succession of ever more extreme measures against the authority and beliefs of the traditional Catholic Church.

In 1535 Henry commissioned a survey of the wealth of 'his' church – the *Valor Ecclesiasticus* ('church valuation') – the first time that the net wealth of the monasteries had been assessed.

In 1536 parliament approved the suppression of two hundred of the smaller and poorer houses, including Waverley which had an income of £174 and Tintern with its income of £192. More closures followed when monks in some northern monasteries joined an uprising in 1537 known as 'the Pilgrimage of Grace' protesting against government policies. The abbots of Whalley and Jervaulx (Cistercian: Yorkshire), were executed as a warning to others who aided rebellion.

Over the next few years the king's chief minister, Thomas Cromwell (c. 1485–1540), employed a range of tactics to persuade the remaining abbots to 'voluntarily' surrender their properties to the crown. These ranged from terror and the discrediting of monastic reputations, to pay-offs and generous pensions for those who co-operated and went quietly. None of this would have been as easy if monasticism had enjoyed deep-rooted public support, but this had been gradually evaporating over the preceding

Opposite: The thirteenth-century interior of Dore Abbey looking towards the north transept (Cistercian: Abbey Dore, Herefordshire).

Thomas Cromwell
(*c.* 1485–1540),
after a painting
by Hans Holbein.

centuries as fewer people became monks, benefactors endowed other institutions (including their own churches), and individualism became more assertive. Jealousy over their wealth and Protestant hostility to miracle-working shrines added to their isolation.

Some abbots and monks made the best of their new circumstances and changed sides – a few more than once. When Osney (Oseney) Abbey (Augustinian: Oxford) was dissolved in 1539 the last abbot, Robert King (d. 1558), a former Cistercian monk, became the bishop of a new – and very short-lived – Protestant diocese known as Thame and Oseney with the abbey converted to a Cathedral. Three years later following another reorganisation he became the first Bishop of Oxford after a different former Augustinian priory in the city was raised to Cathedral status in 1545 and Oseney Abbey demoted. Ten years later, however, he reverted to Catholicism and served as one of the judges who sentenced Archbishop Thomas Cranmer (1489–1556), a leading figure in the English Reformation, to death. A window in Christ Church Cathedral, Oxford, painted around 1630–40, shows Bishop King standing beside an image of the now lost abbey of Oseney.

Oxford was not the only new Cathedral diocese centred around a former abbey church: Chester and Gloucester also survived for the same reason.

Bishop Robert
King with
Oseney Abbey
shown at the
lower left side
of the window,
Christ Church
Cathedral, Oxford,
1630–40.

Most buildings, however, were not so lucky and were sold for salvage with their roofs stripped and their walls quarried for stone. At Quarr Abbey (Cistercian: Isle of Wight), for example, the stone was used to build coastal forts at Cowes. Monastic graves were also robbed, as at Rievaulx, where tombs in the chapter house appear to have been dug up and the bones scattered. In other instances, parts of the buildings survived when a local town bought the church for parish use (at Malmesbury, Pershore (Benedictine: Worcestershire), Sherborne and Tewkesbury, for example), or when they were restored by individuals (Dore Abbey – Cistercian: Herefordshire) or converted into country estates for wealthy Tudors, as at Forde Abbey and Lacock Abbey (Augustinian nunnery: Wiltshire). As a result some have survived as lively centres of enduring Christian worship.

But perhaps it is as ruins that most medieval monasteries are remembered today; evocative monuments of a way of life which continues to intrigue present-day visitors as much as it did four hundred years ago when the playwright, John Webster (c. 1580–c. 1634) wrote:

> I do love these ancient ruins.
> We never tread upon them, but we set
> Our foot upon some reverend history.

Left: The nave of Malmesbury Abbey (Benedictine: Wiltshire).

Overleaf: The ruins of Rievaulx Abbey (Cistercian: Yorkshire).

FURTHER READING

Banham, Debby. *Monasteriales Indicia: The Anglo-Saxon Monastic Sign Language*. Anglo-Saxon Books, 1991 and reprints.

Brooke, Christopher. *The Age of the Cloister*. Hidden Spring, 2003.

Bruce, Scott G. *Silence and Sign Language in Medieval Monasticism: The Cluniac Tradition c.900–1200*. Cambridge University Press, 2007.

Burton, Janet E. *Monastic and Religious Orders in Britain, 1000–1130*. Cambridge University Press, 1994.

Burton, Janet E. *The Monastic Order in Yorkshire 1066–1215*. Cambridge University Press, 1999 and reprints.

Burton, Janet E. and Julie Kerr. *The Cistercians in the Middle Ages*. Boydell Press, 2011.

Clark, James G. (ed.) *The Culture of Medieval English Monasticism*. Boydell Press, 2007.

Clark, James G. *The Benedictines in the Middle Ages*. Boydell Press, 2011.

Connor, Meriel. *John Stone's Chronicle, Christ Church Priory, Canterbury 1417–1472*. Western Michigan University, 2010.

Coppack, Glyn and Mick Aston. *Christ's Poor Men: The Carthusians in England*. NPI Media Group, 2002.

Coppack, Glyn. *Fountains Abbey: The Cistercians in Northern England*. Amberley Publishing, 2009.

Coppack, Glyn. *Abbeys and Priories*. Stroud, 2009.

Coppack, Glyn. *The White Monks: The Cistercians in Britain 1128–1540*. The History Press, 1998.

Cowley, F. G. *The Monastic Order in South Wales, 1066–1349*. University of Wales Press, 1977.

Gilchrist, Roberta. *Gender and Material culture: The Archaeology of Religious Women*. Routledge, 1994.

Gilchrist, Roberta and Barney Sloane. *Requiem: The Medieval Monastic Cemetery in Britain*. Museum of London Archaeology Service, 2005.

Greene, J. Patrick. *Medieval Monasteries*. Continuum, 2005.

Harvey, Barbara F. *Living and Dying in England, 1100–1540: The Monastic Experience*. Oxford University Press, 1993 and reprints.

Heale, Martin. *Monasticism in Late Medieval England c.1300–1535* (selected sources translated and annotated). Manchester University Press, 2009.

Kerr, Julie. *Monastic Hospitality: The Benedictines in England, c.1070–c.1250*. Boydell Press, 2007.

Kerr, Julie. *Life in the Medieval Cloister*. Continuum, 2009.

Knowles, David. *The Religious Orders in England*. 3 Vols. Cambridge University Press, 1948–61 and reprints.

Knowles, David. *The Monastic Order in England: 943–1216*. Cambridge University Press, 1966.

Lawrence, C.H. *Medieval Monasticism*. Longman, 2001.

Luxford, J. (ed.) *Studies in Carthusian Monasticism in the Late Middle Ages*. Brepols, 2008.

Luxford, J. *The Art and Architecture of English Benedictine Monasteries, 1300–1540: A Patronage History*. Boydell Press, 2005.

Oliva, Marilyn. *The Convent and the Community in Late Medieval England*. Boydell Press, 1998.

Parry, Abbot and Esther de Waal. *The Rule of St Benedict*. Gracewing, 1990 and reprints.

Platt, Colin. *The Abbeys and Priories of Medieval England*. Secker and Warburg, 1984.

Power, Eileen. *Medieval English Nunneries, c.1275 to 1535*. Cambridge University Press, 1922.

Robinson, David M. (ed.) *The Cistercian Abbeys of Britain*. Cistercian Publications, 1998.

Robinson, M. David. *The Cistercians in Wales: Architecture and Archaeology 1130–1540*. Oxbow Books, 2006.

Sherlock, David. *Signs for Silence*. Ely Cathedral Publications, 1992.

Stöber, Karen. *Late Medieval Monasteries and their Patrons: England and Wales, c.1300–1540*. Boydell Press, 2007.

Thompson, E. Margaret. *A History of the Somerset Carthusians*. London, 1895.

Williams, David. H. *The Welsh Cistercians*. Gracewing, 2001.

Wright, Geoffrey N. *Discovering Abbeys and Priories*. Shire Publications, 1969 and reprints.

Youings, Joyce. *The Dissolution of the Monasteries*. Allen & Unwin, 1972.

Zarnecki, George. *The Monastic Achievement*. McGraw-Hill, 1972.

WEBSITES

www.cadw.wales.gov.uk
www.cistercians.shef.ac.uk
www.english-heritage.org.uk
www.monasticwales.org
www.vidimus.org

PLACES TO VISIT

Please check opening hours before making long journeys.

ENGLAND

BEDFORDSHIRE
Dunstable Priory (Augustinian): church in use.

BERKSHIRE
Reading Abbey (Cluniac): church demolished, ruins of chapter house, restored gatehouse; local museum has a collection of carved capitals.

CAMBRIDGESHIRE
Denny Abbey (Benedictine and Franciscan nuns): includes remains of monastic church and buildings. English Heritage.
Ely Cathedral Priory (Benedictine): church and some monastic buildings including Prior Crauden's chapel (1324) and gatehouse.
Peterborough Cathedral (Benedictine): abbey church and some monastic buildings.

CHESHIRE
Birkenhead Priory (Benedictine): chapter house in use as a chapel; other monastic remains and museum.
Chester Cathedral (Benedictine): former abbey church and cloisters with chapter house and refectory.
Norton Priory (Augustinian): church demolished, monastic remains and museum. Norton Priory Museum Trust.

CORNWALL
St Germain's Chapel (Augustinian): church in use.

CUMBRIA
Carlisle Cathedral (Augustinian): church, some monastic buildings and gatehouse.
Cartmel Priory (Augustinian): church and monastic gatehouse.
Furness Abbey (Cistercian): extensive ruins including chapter house. English Heritage.
Lanercost Priory (Augustinian): Extensive ruins with preserved undercroft. English Heritage.
Shap Abbey (Premonstratensian): ruins. English Heritage.

DEVON

Torre Abbey (Premonstratensian): church demolished; later house incorporates monastic buildings. Torbay Council.

DORSET

Christchurch Priory (Augustinian): church in use.

Ford Abbey (Cistercian): house open to the public incorporating monastic remains, including lay brothers' dorter.

Shaftesbury Abbey (Benedictine nunnery: some ruins and attached museum. Shaftesbury Abbey Museum and Garden Trust.

Sherborne Abbey (Benedictine): church in use.

DURHAM

Durham Cathedral (Benedictine): church and good monastic buildings.

Finchale Priory (Benedictine): extensive ruins. English Heritage.

ESSEX

Waltham Abbey (Augustinian): church in use, monastic gatehouse.

GLOUCESTERSHIRE

Bristol Cathedral (Augustinian): church and some monastic buildings.

Gloucester Cathedral (Benedictine): church and monastic cloisters.

Hailes Abbey (Cistercian): ruins and museum. English Heritage.

Tewkesbury Abbey (Benedictine): church and monastic gatehouse.

HAMPSHIRE

Beaulieu Abbey (Cistercian): privately owned house and garden incorporating monastic ruins and lay brothers' dorter. Former monastic refectory converted to parish church.

Netley Abbey (Cistercian): extensive ruins. English Heritage.

Romsey Abbey (Benedictine nunnery): church in use.

Titchfield Abbey (Premonstratensian): monastic gatehouse and ruins. English Heritage.

Winchester Cathedral (Benedictine): church, few monastic remains.

HEREFORDSHIRE

Dore Abbey (Cistercian): church in use.

Leominster Priory (Benedictine): church in use.

HERTFORDSHIRE

St Albans Cathedral (Benedictine): church and monastic gatehouse.

KENT

Canterbury Cathedral (Benedictine): church and monastic buildings.

Canterbury, St Augustine's Abbey (Benedictine): extensive ruins and gatehouse. English Heritage.

Minster-in-Sheppey Priory (Benedictine nunnery): church in use, monastic gatehouse.

Rochester Cathedral (Benedictine): church and some monastic buildings.

LANCASHIRE

Sawley Abbey (Cistercian): extensive ruins. English Heritage.

Whalley Abbey (Cistercian): extensive ruins and gatehouses. Diocese of Blackburn.

LINCOLNSHIRE

Croyland (Crowland) Abbey (Benedictine): church in use with adjacent ruins.

Thornton Abbey (Augustinian): church demolished, monastic gatehouse. English Heritage.

LONDON

Bishopsgate, St Helen's (Benedictine nunnery): church in use.

Smithfield Priory (Augustinian): church in use, east cloister walk and gatehouse.

Southwark Cathedral (Augustinian): church in use, no monastic remains.

Westminster Abbey (Benedictine): church and monastic cloisters, octagonal chapter house with tiled floor and wall paintings.

NORFOLK

Binham Priory (Benedictine): church in use, monastic ruins.

Castle Acre Priory (Cluniac): church demolished, extensive ruins, Prior's House. English Heritage.

Norwich Cathedral (Benedictine): church in use, monastic cloisters and gatehouse.

Thetford Priory (Cluniac): extensive ruins, monastic gatehouse. English Heritage.

Wymondham Abbey (Benedictine): church in use.

NORTHUMBERLAND

Brinkburn Priory (Augustinian): restored church and some monastic buildings. English Heritage.

Hexham Priory (Augustinian): church in use, some monastic remains.

Lindisfarne Priory (Benedictine): extensive ruins. English Heritage.

Tynemouth Priory (Benedictine): extensive ruins. English Heritage.

NOTTINGHAMSHIRE

Newstead Priory (Augustinian): monastic remains within private house. Nottingham City Council.

Worksop Priory (Augustinian): church in use, monastic gatehouse.

OXFORDSHIRE

Abingdon Abbey (Benedictine): church demolished, some monastic buildings including gatehouse.

Dorchester Abbey (Augustinian): church in use, with museum.

Oxford, Christ Church Cathedral (Augustinian): church in use, chapter house, cloister walks.

SHROPSHIRE

Buildwas Abbey (Cistercian): extensive ruins with monastic chapter house and undercrofts. English Heritage.

Haughmond Abbey (Augustinian): extensive ruins with chapter house. English Heritage.

Lilleshall Abbey (Augustinian): extensive ruins.

Shrewsbury Abbey (Benedictine): church in use, refectory pulpit in nearby public garden.

Wenlock Priory (Cluniac): extensive ruins. English Heritage.

SOMERSET

Bath Abbey (Benedictine): church in use.

Cleeve Abbey (Cistercian): extensive ruins including refectory, dormitory, chapter house and gatehouse. English Heritage.

Glastonbury Abbey (Benedictine): extensive ruins with well-preserved medieval kitchen, abbey gatehouse and museum. Glastonbury Abbey Trust.

Muchelney Abbey (Benedictine): church demolished, well-preserved Abbot's lodgings, separate latrine block. English Heritage.

Witham Priory (Carthusian): church in use.

STAFFORDSHIRE

Croxden Abbey (Cistercian): extensive ruins. English Heritage.

SUFFOLK

Bury St Edmunds Abbey (Benedictine): fragmented ruins, fine gatehouse.

Leiston Abbey (Premonstratensian): extensive ruins. English Heritage.

SURREY

Waverley Abbey (Cistercian): ruins include vaulted cellar. English Heritage.

SUSSEX

Battle Abbey (Benedictine): gatehouse, undercroft and other ruins.
   English Heritage.
Bayham Abbey (Premonstratensian): extensive ruins. English Heritage.
Boxgrove Priory (Benedictine): church in use and some monastic remains.
Lewes Priory (Cluniac): extensive ruins. Lewes Priory Trust.
Michelham Priory (Augustinian): gatehouse and other monastic buildings.
   Sussex Archaeological Society.

WARWICKSHIRE

Coventry Cathedral Priory (Benedictine): church and monastery
   demolished but excavations and museum at Priory Visitors' Centre.
Merevale Abbey (Cistercian): gatehouse chapel in use as parish church.

WILTSHIRE

Lacock Abbey (Augustinian nunnery): monastic remains incorporated into
   house including cloister, chapter house, and day room. National Trust.
Malmesbury Abbey (Benedictine): church in use.

WORCESTERSHIRE

Evesham Abbey (Benedictine): church demolished; bell tower, almonry
   (now tourist office/museum).
Great Malvern Priory (Benedictine): church in use, good collection
   of stained glass; museum in monastic gatehouse.
Pershore Abbey (Benedictine): church in use.
Worcester Cathedral (Benedictine): church, monastic cloisters,
   chapter house.

YORKSHIRE

Bolton Priory (Augustinian): church in use, extensive ruins.
Bridlington Priory (Augustinian): church in use, monastic gatehouse.
Byland Abbey (Cistercian): extensive ruins including tiled pavement.
   English Heritage.
Easby Abbey (Premonstratensian): extensive ruins. English Heritage.
Fountains Abbey (Cistercian): extensive ruins, large vaulted cellar.
   National Trust.
Guisborough Priory (Augustinian): spectacular ruins. English Heritage.
Jervaulx Abbey (Cistercian): extensive ruins. Private ownership,
   free admission.

Kirkham Priory (Augustinian): extensive ruins, monastic gatehouse.
    English Heritage.
Kirkstall Abbey (Cistercian): extensive ruins with museum. Leeds
    Museums and Galleries.
Monk Bretton Priory (Cluniac): ruins with gatehouses. English Heritage.
Mount Grace Priory (Carthusian): shell of church, extensive ruins,
    reconstructed monk's cell. English Heritage.
Rievaulx Abbey (Cistercian): extensive ruins with museum.
    English Heritage.
Roche Abbey (Cistercian): extensive ruins. English Heritage.
Selby Abbey (Benedictine): church in use.
Whitby Abbey (Benedictine): extensive ruins of church.
York, St Mary's Abbey (Benedictine): extensive ruins, finds in
    city museum.

WALES

CEREDIGION
Strata Florida Abbey (Cistercian): extensive ruins. Cadw.

DENBIGHSHIRE
Valle Crucis Abbey (Cistercian): extensive ruins with chapter house
    and dormitory above. Cadw.

FLINTSHIRE
Basingwerk Abbey (Cistercian): ruins of chapter house and monastic
    refectory. Cadw.

GLAMORGAN
Ewenny Priory (Benedictine): church in use, gatehouses.

MONMOUTHSHIRE
Llanthony Priory (Augustinian): extensive ruins. Cadw.
Tintern Abbey (Cistercian): extensive ruins. Cadw.

POWYS
Brecon Cathedral (Benedictine): church in use, no monastic remains.

INDEX